50 Premium Smoothie Recipes for Home

By: Kelly Johnson

Table of Contents

- Strawberry Chia Smoothie
- Mango Lime Smoothie
- Pineapple Kale Smoothie
- Chocolate Cherry Smoothie
- Peach Blueberry Smoothie
- Green Apple Smoothie
- Spiced Pear Smoothie
- Almond Joy Smoothie
- Coconut Pineapple Smoothie
- Berry Protein Smoothie
- Kiwi Coconut Smoothie
- Avocado Pineapple Smoothie
- Berry Citrus Smoothie
- Ginger Peach Smoothie

Berry Banana Smoothie

Ingredients:

- 1 banana (fresh or frozen)
- 1 cup (150 g) mixed berries (such as strawberries, blueberries, raspberries, or blackberries, fresh or frozen)
- 1 cup (240 ml) milk (any kind: dairy or non-dairy like almond, soy, or oat milk)
- 1/2 cup (120 ml) Greek yogurt (plain or vanilla)
- 1-2 tablespoons honey or maple syrup (optional, adjust to taste)
- 1/2 teaspoon vanilla extract (optional)
- 1/2 cup ice (if using fresh fruit or if you prefer a colder smoothie)

Instructions:

1. **Prepare the Ingredients:**
   - If using fresh berries, rinse them thoroughly. If using frozen berries, no need to thaw them.
2. **Blend:**
   - In a blender, combine the banana, mixed berries, milk, Greek yogurt, honey or maple syrup (if using), and vanilla extract (if using).
3. **Add Ice:**
   - Add ice if you're using fresh fruit or if you prefer a colder, thicker smoothie.
4. **Blend Until Smooth:**
   - Blend on high speed until the mixture is smooth and creamy. If the smoothie is too thick, you can add a little more milk to reach your desired consistency.
5. **Taste and Adjust:**
   - Taste the smoothie and adjust sweetness if needed by adding more honey or maple syrup.
6. **Serve:**
   - Pour the smoothie into glasses and serve immediately.

Enjoy your refreshing and nutritious Berry Banana Smoothie!

Mango Pineapple Smoothie

Ingredients:

- 1 cup (150 g) frozen mango chunks
- 1 cup (150 g) frozen pineapple chunks
- 1 cup (240 ml) orange juice or coconut water
- 1/2 cup (120 ml) Greek yogurt (plain or vanilla) or non-dairy yogurt
- 1 tablespoon honey or maple syrup (optional, adjust to taste)
- 1/2 teaspoon vanilla extract (optional)
- 1/2 cup ice (optional, if you want a thicker smoothie)

Instructions:

1. **Prepare the Ingredients:**
   - Measure out the frozen mango and pineapple chunks. If you're using fresh fruit, add 1/2 cup of ice to the blender for a colder, thicker texture.
2. **Blend:**
   - In a blender, combine the frozen mango, frozen pineapple, orange juice or coconut water, Greek yogurt, honey or maple syrup (if using), and vanilla extract (if using).
3. **Add Ice:**
   - Add ice if using fresh fruit or if you prefer a colder smoothie.
4. **Blend Until Smooth:**
   - Blend on high speed until the mixture is smooth and creamy. If the smoothie is too thick, you can add a bit more orange juice or coconut water to reach your desired consistency.
5. **Taste and Adjust:**
   - Taste the smoothie and adjust sweetness if needed by adding more honey or maple syrup.
6. **Serve:**
   - Pour the smoothie into glasses and serve immediately.

Enjoy your tropical Mango Pineapple Smoothie!

Green Kale Smoothie

Ingredients:

- 1 cup (60 g) kale leaves (stems removed and chopped)
- 1 banana (fresh or frozen)
- 1/2 cup (120 ml) apple juice or coconut water
- 1/2 cup (120 ml) Greek yogurt (plain or vanilla) or non-dairy yogurt
- 1/2 cup (80 g) frozen pineapple chunks
- 1/2 cup (80 g) frozen mango chunks
- 1 tablespoon honey or maple syrup (optional, adjust to taste)
- 1/2 teaspoon lemon juice (optional)
- 1/2 cup ice (optional, if you prefer a colder smoothie)

Instructions:

1. **Prepare the Ingredients:**
   - Wash and chop the kale, remove the stems, and peel the banana. If you're using fresh fruit, add 1/2 cup of ice for a thicker, colder smoothie.
2. **Blend:**
   - In a blender, combine the kale, banana, apple juice or coconut water, Greek yogurt, frozen pineapple chunks, and frozen mango chunks.
3. **Add Sweetener and Lemon Juice:**
   - Add honey or maple syrup if you prefer a sweeter smoothie. You can also add lemon juice for a hint of tartness.
4. **Add Ice (if needed):**
   - If you're using fresh fruit or want a colder smoothie, add ice to the blender.
5. **Blend Until Smooth:**
   - Blend on high speed until the mixture is smooth and creamy. Adjust the consistency by adding more apple juice or coconut water if needed.
6. **Taste and Adjust:**
   - Taste the smoothie and adjust sweetness or tartness as needed by adding more honey/maple syrup or lemon juice.
7. **Serve:**
   - Pour the smoothie into glasses and serve immediately.

Enjoy your healthy and energizing Green Kale Smoothie!

Strawberry Avocado Smoothie

Ingredients:

- 1 cup (150 g) fresh or frozen strawberries
- 1/2 ripe avocado
- 1 cup (240 ml) milk (any kind: dairy or non-dairy like almond, soy, or oat milk)
- 1/2 cup (120 ml) Greek yogurt (plain or vanilla) or non-dairy yogurt
- 1-2 tablespoons honey or maple syrup (optional, adjust to taste)
- 1/2 teaspoon vanilla extract (optional)
- 1/2 cup ice (optional, if using fresh fruit or if you prefer a colder smoothie)

Instructions:

1. **Prepare the Ingredients:**
   - If using fresh strawberries, wash and hull them. If using frozen strawberries, you can skip this step. Cut the avocado in half, remove the pit, and scoop out the flesh.
2. **Blend:**
   - In a blender, combine the strawberries, avocado, milk, Greek yogurt, and optional honey or maple syrup. Add the vanilla extract if desired.
3. **Add Ice (if needed):**
   - If you're using fresh fruit or want a thicker, colder smoothie, add ice to the blender.
4. **Blend Until Smooth:**
   - Blend on high speed until the mixture is smooth and creamy. Adjust the consistency by adding more milk if needed.
5. **Taste and Adjust:**
   - Taste the smoothie and adjust sweetness if needed by adding more honey or maple syrup.
6. **Serve:**
   - Pour the smoothie into glasses and serve immediately.

Enjoy your creamy and refreshing Strawberry Avocado Smoothie!

Peach Almond Smoothie

Ingredients:

- 1 cup (150 g) fresh or frozen peach slices
- 1/4 cup (30 g) almonds (toasted or raw, but toasted adds extra flavor)
- 1 cup (240 ml) almond milk (or any milk of your choice)
- 1/2 cup (120 ml) Greek yogurt (plain or vanilla) or non-dairy yogurt
- 1 tablespoon honey or maple syrup (optional, adjust to taste)
- 1/2 teaspoon vanilla extract (optional)
- 1/2 cup ice (optional, if using fresh fruit or if you prefer a colder smoothie)

Instructions:

1. **Prepare the Ingredients:**
   - If using fresh peaches, peel and slice them. If using frozen peaches, you can skip this step. If using raw almonds, consider toasting them for extra flavor by lightly roasting them in a pan over medium heat for a few minutes.
2. **Blend:**
   - In a blender, combine the peach slices, almonds, almond milk, Greek yogurt, and optional honey or maple syrup. Add the vanilla extract if desired.
3. **Add Ice (if needed):**
   - If you're using fresh peaches or want a thicker, colder smoothie, add ice to the blender.
4. **Blend Until Smooth:**
   - Blend on high speed until the mixture is smooth and creamy. Adjust the consistency by adding more almond milk if needed.
5. **Taste and Adjust:**
   - Taste the smoothie and adjust sweetness if needed by adding more honey or maple syrup.
6. **Serve:**
   - Pour the smoothie into glasses and serve immediately.

Enjoy your flavorful and creamy Peach Almond Smoothie!

Chocolate Banana Smoothie

Ingredients:

- 1 banana (fresh or frozen)
- 1 cup (240 ml) milk (any kind: dairy or non-dairy like almond, soy, or oat milk)
- 2 tablespoons cocoa powder (unsweetened)
- 2 tablespoons chocolate syrup or chocolate chips (optional, for extra chocolate flavor)
- 1/2 cup (120 ml) Greek yogurt (plain or vanilla) or non-dairy yogurt
- 1 tablespoon honey or maple syrup (optional, adjust to taste)
- 1/2 teaspoon vanilla extract (optional)
- 1/2 cup ice (optional, if using fresh fruit or if you prefer a colder smoothie)

Instructions:

1. **Prepare the Ingredients:**
   - If using a fresh banana, peel and slice it. If using frozen banana, you can skip this step.
2. **Blend:**
   - In a blender, combine the banana, milk, cocoa powder, chocolate syrup or chocolate chips (if using), Greek yogurt, and optional honey or maple syrup. Add the vanilla extract if desired.
3. **Add Ice (if needed):**
   - If you're using fresh banana or want a thicker, colder smoothie, add ice to the blender.
4. **Blend Until Smooth:**
   - Blend on high speed until the mixture is smooth and creamy. Adjust the consistency by adding more milk if needed.
5. **Taste and Adjust:**
   - Taste the smoothie and adjust sweetness or chocolate flavor if needed by adding more honey, maple syrup, or chocolate syrup/chips.
6. **Serve:**
   - Pour the smoothie into glasses and serve immediately.

Enjoy your creamy and indulgent Chocolate Banana Smoothie!

Tropical Green Smoothie

Ingredients:

- 1 cup (60 g) spinach leaves (fresh or frozen)
- 1/2 cup (80 g) frozen pineapple chunks
- 1/2 cup (80 g) frozen mango chunks
- 1 banana (fresh or frozen)
- 1 cup (240 ml) coconut water or orange juice
- 1/2 cup (120 ml) Greek yogurt (plain or vanilla) or non-dairy yogurt
- 1 tablespoon honey or maple syrup (optional, adjust to taste)
- 1/2 teaspoon vanilla extract (optional)
- 1/2 cup ice (optional, if using fresh fruit or if you prefer a colder smoothie)

Instructions:

1. **Prepare the Ingredients:**
   - If using fresh spinach, wash it thoroughly. Peel and slice the banana. If using fresh fruit, consider adding ice for a colder smoothie.
2. **Blend:**
   - In a blender, combine the spinach, frozen pineapple chunks, frozen mango chunks, banana, coconut water or orange juice, and Greek yogurt.
3. **Add Sweetener and Vanilla:**
   - Add honey or maple syrup if you prefer a sweeter smoothie. Add vanilla extract if desired.
4. **Add Ice (if needed):**
   - If using fresh fruit or if you want a thicker, colder smoothie, add ice to the blender.
5. **Blend Until Smooth:**
   - Blend on high speed until the mixture is smooth and creamy. Adjust the consistency by adding more coconut water or orange juice if needed.
6. **Taste and Adjust:**
   - Taste the smoothie and adjust sweetness if needed by adding more honey or maple syrup.
7. **Serve:**
   - Pour the smoothie into glasses and serve immediately.

Enjoy your tropical and refreshing Tropical Green Smoothie!

Chocolate Banana Smoothie

Ingredients:

- 1 banana (fresh or frozen)
- 1 cup (240 ml) milk (any kind: dairy or non-dairy like almond, soy, or oat milk)
- 2 tablespoons cocoa powder (unsweetened)
- 2 tablespoons chocolate syrup or chocolate chips (optional, for extra chocolate flavor)
- 1/2 cup (120 ml) Greek yogurt (plain or vanilla) or non-dairy yogurt
- 1 tablespoon honey or maple syrup (optional, adjust to taste)
- 1/2 teaspoon vanilla extract (optional)
- 1/2 cup ice (optional, if using fresh fruit or if you prefer a colder smoothie)

Instructions:

1. **Prepare the Ingredients:**
   - If using a fresh banana, peel and slice it. If using frozen banana, you can skip this step.
2. **Blend:**
   - In a blender, combine the banana, milk, cocoa powder, chocolate syrup or chocolate chips (if using), Greek yogurt, and optional honey or maple syrup. Add the vanilla extract if desired.
3. **Add Ice (if needed):**
   - If you're using fresh banana or want a thicker, colder smoothie, add ice to the blender.
4. **Blend Until Smooth:**
   - Blend on high speed until the mixture is smooth and creamy. Adjust the consistency by adding more milk if needed.
5. **Taste and Adjust:**
   - Taste the smoothie and adjust sweetness or chocolate flavor if needed by adding more honey, maple syrup, or chocolate syrup/chips.
6. **Serve:**
   - Pour the smoothie into glasses and serve immediately.

Enjoy your creamy and indulgent Chocolate Banana Smoothie!

Tropical Green Smoothie

Ingredients:

- 1 cup (60 g) spinach leaves (fresh or frozen)
- 1/2 cup (80 g) frozen pineapple chunks
- 1/2 cup (80 g) frozen mango chunks
- 1 banana (fresh or frozen)
- 1 cup (240 ml) coconut water or orange juice
- 1/2 cup (120 ml) Greek yogurt (plain or vanilla) or non-dairy yogurt
- 1 tablespoon honey or maple syrup (optional, adjust to taste)
- 1/2 teaspoon vanilla extract (optional)
- 1/2 cup ice (optional, if using fresh fruit or if you prefer a colder smoothie)

Instructions:

1. **Prepare the Ingredients:**
   - If using fresh spinach, wash it thoroughly. Peel and slice the banana. If using fresh fruit, consider adding ice for a colder smoothie.
2. **Blend:**
   - In a blender, combine the spinach, frozen pineapple chunks, frozen mango chunks, banana, coconut water or orange juice, and Greek yogurt.
3. **Add Sweetener and Vanilla:**
   - Add honey or maple syrup if you prefer a sweeter smoothie. Add vanilla extract if desired.
4. **Add Ice (if needed):**
   - If using fresh fruit or if you want a thicker, colder smoothie, add ice to the blender.
5. **Blend Until Smooth:**
   - Blend on high speed until the mixture is smooth and creamy. Adjust the consistency by adding more coconut water or orange juice if needed.
6. **Taste and Adjust:**
   - Taste the smoothie and adjust sweetness if needed by adding more honey or maple syrup.
7. **Serve:**
   - Pour the smoothie into glasses and serve immediately.

Enjoy your tropical and refreshing Tropical Green Smoothie!

Blueberry Spinach Smoothie

Ingredients:

- 1 cup (60 g) fresh or frozen spinach leaves
- 1 cup (150 g) fresh or frozen blueberries
- 1 banana (fresh or frozen)
- 1 cup (240 ml) almond milk (or any milk of your choice)
- 1/2 cup (120 ml) Greek yogurt (plain or vanilla) or non-dairy yogurt
- 1 tablespoon honey or maple syrup (optional, adjust to taste)
- 1/2 teaspoon vanilla extract (optional)
- 1/2 cup ice (optional, if using fresh fruit or if you prefer a colder smoothie)

Instructions:

1. **Prepare the Ingredients:**
   - Wash the spinach leaves thoroughly. If using fresh blueberries, rinse them. Peel and slice the banana. If using fresh fruit, consider adding ice for a colder smoothie.
2. **Blend:**
   - In a blender, combine the spinach, blueberries, banana, almond milk, and Greek yogurt.
3. **Add Sweetener and Vanilla:**
   - Add honey or maple syrup if you prefer a sweeter smoothie. Add vanilla extract if desired.
4. **Add Ice (if needed):**
   - If using fresh fruit or if you want a thicker, colder smoothie, add ice to the blender.
5. **Blend Until Smooth:**
   - Blend on high speed until the mixture is smooth and creamy. Adjust the consistency by adding more almond milk if needed.
6. **Taste and Adjust:**
   - Taste the smoothie and adjust sweetness if needed by adding more honey or maple syrup.
7. **Serve:**
   - Pour the smoothie into glasses and serve immediately.

Enjoy your healthy and delicious Blueberry Spinach Smoothie!

Raspberry Kiwi Smoothie

Ingredients:

- 1 cup (150 g) fresh or frozen raspberries
- 2 ripe kiwis, peeled and sliced
- 1 banana (fresh or frozen)
- 1 cup (240 ml) coconut water or apple juice
- 1/2 cup (120 ml) Greek yogurt (plain or vanilla) or non-dairy yogurt
- 1 tablespoon honey or maple syrup (optional, adjust to taste)
- 1/2 teaspoon vanilla extract (optional)
- 1/2 cup ice (optional, if using fresh fruit or if you prefer a colder smoothie)

Instructions:

1. **Prepare the Ingredients:**
   - If using fresh raspberries, rinse them thoroughly. Peel and slice the kiwis. Peel and slice the banana. If using fresh fruit, add ice for a thicker, colder smoothie.
2. **Blend:**
   - In a blender, combine the raspberries, kiwis, banana, coconut water or apple juice, and Greek yogurt.
3. **Add Sweetener and Vanilla:**
   - Add honey or maple syrup if you prefer a sweeter smoothie. Add vanilla extract if desired.
4. **Add Ice (if needed):**
   - If using fresh fruit or if you want a colder smoothie, add ice to the blender.
5. **Blend Until Smooth:**
   - Blend on high speed until the mixture is smooth and creamy. Adjust the consistency by adding more coconut water or apple juice if needed.
6. **Taste and Adjust:**
   - Taste the smoothie and adjust sweetness if needed by adding more honey or maple syrup.
7. **Serve:**
   - Pour the smoothie into glasses and serve immediately.

Enjoy your refreshing and tangy Raspberry Kiwi Smoothie!

Apple Cinnamon Smoothie

Ingredients:

- 1 apple (peeled, cored, and sliced; any variety you prefer)
- 1 banana (fresh or frozen)
- 1/2 cup (120 ml) Greek yogurt (plain or vanilla) or non-dairy yogurt
- 1 cup (240 ml) milk (any kind: dairy or non-dairy like almond, soy, or oat milk)
- 1/2 teaspoon ground cinnamon
- 1 tablespoon honey or maple syrup (optional, adjust to taste)
- 1/2 teaspoon vanilla extract (optional)
- 1/2 cup ice (optional, if using fresh fruit or if you prefer a colder smoothie)

Instructions:

1. **Prepare the Ingredients:**
   - Peel, core, and slice the apple. If using fresh fruit, consider adding ice for a colder, thicker smoothie. Peel and slice the banana.
2. **Blend:**
   - In a blender, combine the apple slices, banana, Greek yogurt, milk, and ground cinnamon.
3. **Add Sweetener and Vanilla:**
   - Add honey or maple syrup if you prefer a sweeter smoothie. Add vanilla extract if desired.
4. **Add Ice (if needed):**
   - If using fresh fruit or if you want a colder smoothie, add ice to the blender.
5. **Blend Until Smooth:**
   - Blend on high speed until the mixture is smooth and creamy. Adjust the consistency by adding more milk if needed.
6. **Taste and Adjust:**
   - Taste the smoothie and adjust sweetness or cinnamon flavor if needed by adding more honey/maple syrup or cinnamon.
7. **Serve:**
   - Pour the smoothie into glasses and serve immediately.

Enjoy your cozy and flavorful Apple Cinnamon Smoothie!

Coffee Banana Smoothie

Ingredients:

- 1 banana (fresh or frozen)
- 1 cup (240 ml) brewed coffee (cooled or chilled)
- 1/2 cup (120 ml) Greek yogurt (plain or vanilla) or non-dairy yogurt
- 1/2 cup (120 ml) milk (any kind: dairy or non-dairy like almond, soy, or oat milk)
- 1-2 tablespoons honey or maple syrup (optional, adjust to taste)
- 1/2 teaspoon vanilla extract (optional)
- 1/2 cup ice (optional, if using fresh banana or if you prefer a colder smoothie)

Instructions:

1. **Prepare the Ingredients:**
   - If using fresh banana, peel and slice it. Brew and cool your coffee ahead of time. If using frozen banana, you can skip this step. If using fresh fruit, consider adding ice for a thicker, colder smoothie.
2. **Blend:**
   - In a blender, combine the banana, brewed coffee, Greek yogurt, milk, and optional honey or maple syrup. Add vanilla extract if desired.
3. **Add Ice (if needed):**
   - If using fresh banana or if you prefer a colder smoothie, add ice to the blender.
4. **Blend Until Smooth:**
   - Blend on high speed until the mixture is smooth and creamy. Adjust the consistency by adding more milk if needed.
5. **Taste and Adjust:**
   - Taste the smoothie and adjust sweetness if needed by adding more honey or maple syrup.
6. **Serve:**
   - Pour the smoothie into glasses and serve immediately.

Enjoy your energizing and creamy Coffee Banana Smoothie!

Apple Cinnamon Smoothie

Ingredients:

- 1 apple (peeled, cored, and sliced; any variety you prefer)
- 1 banana (fresh or frozen)
- 1/2 cup (120 ml) Greek yogurt (plain or vanilla) or non-dairy yogurt
- 1 cup (240 ml) milk (any kind: dairy or non-dairy like almond, soy, or oat milk)
- 1/2 teaspoon ground cinnamon
- 1 tablespoon honey or maple syrup (optional, adjust to taste)
- 1/2 teaspoon vanilla extract (optional)
- 1/2 cup ice (optional, if using fresh fruit or if you prefer a colder smoothie)

Instructions:

1. **Prepare the Ingredients:**
   - Peel, core, and slice the apple. If using fresh fruit, consider adding ice for a colder, thicker smoothie. Peel and slice the banana.
2. **Blend:**
   - In a blender, combine the apple slices, banana, Greek yogurt, milk, and ground cinnamon.
3. **Add Sweetener and Vanilla:**
   - Add honey or maple syrup if you prefer a sweeter smoothie. Add vanilla extract if desired.
4. **Add Ice (if needed):**
   - If using fresh fruit or if you want a colder smoothie, add ice to the blender.
5. **Blend Until Smooth:**
   - Blend on high speed until the mixture is smooth and creamy. Adjust the consistency by adding more milk if needed.
6. **Taste and Adjust:**
   - Taste the smoothie and adjust sweetness or cinnamon flavor if needed by adding more honey/maple syrup or cinnamon.
7. **Serve:**
   - Pour the smoothie into glasses and serve immediately.

Enjoy your cozy and flavorful Apple Cinnamon Smoothie!

Coffee Banana Smoothie

Ingredients:

- 1 banana (fresh or frozen)
- 1 cup (240 ml) brewed coffee (cooled or chilled)
- 1/2 cup (120 ml) Greek yogurt (plain or vanilla) or non-dairy yogurt
- 1/2 cup (120 ml) milk (any kind: dairy or non-dairy like almond, soy, or oat milk)
- 1-2 tablespoons honey or maple syrup (optional, adjust to taste)
- 1/2 teaspoon vanilla extract (optional)
- 1/2 cup ice (optional, if using fresh banana or if you prefer a colder smoothie)

Instructions:

1. **Prepare the Ingredients:**
   - If using fresh banana, peel and slice it. Brew and cool your coffee ahead of time. If using frozen banana, you can skip this step. If using fresh fruit, consider adding ice for a thicker, colder smoothie.
2. **Blend:**
   - In a blender, combine the banana, brewed coffee, Greek yogurt, milk, and optional honey or maple syrup. Add vanilla extract if desired.
3. **Add Ice (if needed):**
   - If using fresh banana or if you prefer a colder smoothie, add ice to the blender.
4. **Blend Until Smooth:**
   - Blend on high speed until the mixture is smooth and creamy. Adjust the consistency by adding more milk if needed.
5. **Taste and Adjust:**
   - Taste the smoothie and adjust sweetness if needed by adding more honey or maple syrup.
6. **Serve:**
   - Pour the smoothie into glasses and serve immediately.

Enjoy your energizing and creamy Coffee Banana Smoothie!

Orange Mango Smoothie

Ingredients:

- 1 cup (150 g) frozen mango chunks
- 1 orange (peeled and segmented) or 1 cup (240 ml) orange juice
- 1/2 cup (120 ml) Greek yogurt (plain or vanilla) or non-dairy yogurt
- 1/2 cup (120 ml) milk (any kind: dairy or non-dairy like almond, soy, or oat milk)
- 1 tablespoon honey or maple syrup (optional, adjust to taste)
- 1/2 teaspoon vanilla extract (optional)
- 1/2 cup ice (optional, if using fresh fruit or if you prefer a colder smoothie)

Instructions:

1. **Prepare the Ingredients:**
   - Peel and segment the orange if using fresh fruit. If using orange juice, measure out the amount needed. If using fresh mango, consider adding ice for a thicker, colder smoothie.
2. **Blend:**
   - In a blender, combine the frozen mango chunks, orange segments or orange juice, Greek yogurt, and milk.
3. **Add Sweetener and Vanilla:**
   - Add honey or maple syrup if you prefer a sweeter smoothie. Add vanilla extract if desired.
4. **Add Ice (if needed):**
   - If using fresh mango or if you want a colder smoothie, add ice to the blender.
5. **Blend Until Smooth:**
   - Blend on high speed until the mixture is smooth and creamy. Adjust the consistency by adding more milk if needed.
6. **Taste and Adjust:**
   - Taste the smoothie and adjust sweetness if needed by adding more honey or maple syrup.
7. **Serve:**
   - Pour the smoothie into glasses and serve immediately.

Enjoy your refreshing and tropical Orange Mango Smoothie!

Almond Butter Banana Smoothie

Ingredients:

- 1 banana (fresh or frozen)
- 2 tablespoons almond butter
- 1 cup (240 ml) milk (any kind: dairy or non-dairy like almond, soy, or oat milk)
- 1/2 cup (120 ml) Greek yogurt (plain or vanilla) or non-dairy yogurt
- 1 tablespoon honey or maple syrup (optional, adjust to taste)
- 1/2 teaspoon vanilla extract (optional)
- 1/2 cup ice (optional, if using fresh banana or if you prefer a colder smoothie)

Instructions:

1. **Prepare the Ingredients:**
   - If using fresh banana, peel and slice it. If using frozen banana, you can skip this step.
2. **Blend:**
   - In a blender, combine the banana, almond butter, milk, Greek yogurt, and optional honey or maple syrup. Add vanilla extract if desired.
3. **Add Ice (if needed):**
   - If using fresh banana or if you want a thicker, colder smoothie, add ice to the blender.
4. **Blend Until Smooth:**
   - Blend on high speed until the mixture is smooth and creamy. Adjust the consistency by adding more milk if needed.
5. **Taste and Adjust:**
   - Taste the smoothie and adjust sweetness if needed by adding more honey or maple syrup.
6. **Serve:**
   - Pour the smoothie into glasses and serve immediately.

Enjoy your creamy and nutty Almond Butter Banana Smoothie!

Pineapple Coconut Smoothie

Ingredients:

- 1 cup (150 g) frozen pineapple chunks
- 1/2 cup (120 ml) coconut milk (canned or carton, depending on your preference for creaminess)
- 1/2 cup (120 ml) Greek yogurt (plain or vanilla) or non-dairy yogurt
- 1 tablespoon honey or maple syrup (optional, adjust to taste)
- 1/2 teaspoon vanilla extract (optional)
- 1/2 cup ice (optional, if using fresh pineapple or if you prefer a colder smoothie)

Instructions:

1. **Prepare the Ingredients:**
   - If using fresh pineapple, peel, core, and cut it into chunks. If you prefer a thicker smoothie, add ice to the blender.
2. **Blend:**
   - In a blender, combine the frozen pineapple chunks, coconut milk, Greek yogurt, and optional honey or maple syrup. Add vanilla extract if desired.
3. **Add Ice (if needed):**
   - If using fresh pineapple or if you want a thicker, colder smoothie, add ice to the blender.
4. **Blend Until Smooth:**
   - Blend on high speed until the mixture is smooth and creamy. Adjust the consistency by adding more coconut milk if needed.
5. **Taste and Adjust:**
   - Taste the smoothie and adjust sweetness if needed by adding more honey or maple syrup.
6. **Serve:**
   - Pour the smoothie into glasses and serve immediately.

Enjoy your tropical Pineapple Coconut Smoothie!

Chia Seed Berry Smoothie

Ingredients:

- 1 cup (150 g) mixed berries (fresh or frozen; such as strawberries, blueberries, raspberries, and blackberries)
- 1 tablespoon chia seeds
- 1 banana (fresh or frozen)
- 1 cup (240 ml) milk (any kind: dairy or non-dairy like almond, soy, or oat milk)
- 1/2 cup (120 ml) Greek yogurt (plain or vanilla) or non-dairy yogurt
- 1 tablespoon honey or maple syrup (optional, adjust to taste)
- 1/2 teaspoon vanilla extract (optional)
- 1/2 cup ice (optional, if using fresh berries or if you prefer a colder smoothie)

Instructions:

1. **Prepare the Ingredients:**
   - If using fresh berries, rinse them thoroughly. Peel and slice the banana. If using fresh fruit, consider adding ice for a thicker, colder smoothie.
2. **Soak the Chia Seeds:**
   - If you have time, soak the chia seeds in a small amount of water or milk (about 2 tablespoons of liquid) for about 10 minutes to allow them to expand. This step is optional but can help make the smoothie thicker.
3. **Blend:**
   - In a blender, combine the berries, chia seeds, banana, milk, Greek yogurt, and optional honey or maple syrup. Add vanilla extract if desired.
4. **Add Ice (if needed):**
   - If using fresh berries or if you want a thicker, colder smoothie, add ice to the blender.
5. **Blend Until Smooth:**
   - Blend on high speed until the mixture is smooth and creamy. Adjust the consistency by adding more milk if needed.
6. **Taste and Adjust:**
   - Taste the smoothie and adjust sweetness if needed by adding more honey or maple syrup.
7. **Serve:**
   - Pour the smoothie into glasses and serve immediately.

Enjoy your healthy and refreshing Chia Seed Berry Smoothie!

Pumpkin Spice Smoothie

Ingredients:

- 1/2 cup (120 g) canned pumpkin (not pumpkin pie filling)
- 1 banana (fresh or frozen)
- 1 cup (240 ml) milk (any kind: dairy or non-dairy like almond, soy, or oat milk)
- 1/2 cup (120 ml) Greek yogurt (plain or vanilla) or non-dairy yogurt
- 1-2 tablespoons maple syrup or honey (optional, adjust to taste)
- 1/2 teaspoon pumpkin pie spice (or a mix of cinnamon, nutmeg, and ginger)
- 1/2 teaspoon vanilla extract (optional)
- 1/2 cup ice (optional, if using fresh banana or if you prefer a colder smoothie)

Instructions:

1. **Prepare the Ingredients:**
   - If using fresh banana, peel and slice it. If using frozen banana, you can skip this step. If you prefer a thicker smoothie, add ice to the blender.
2. **Blend:**
   - In a blender, combine the canned pumpkin, banana, milk, Greek yogurt, and maple syrup or honey. Add the pumpkin pie spice and vanilla extract if using.
3. **Add Ice (if needed):**
   - If using fresh banana or if you want a thicker, colder smoothie, add ice to the blender.
4. **Blend Until Smooth:**
   - Blend on high speed until the mixture is smooth and creamy. Adjust the consistency by adding more milk if needed.
5. **Taste and Adjust:**
   - Taste the smoothie and adjust sweetness or spice if needed by adding more maple syrup or pumpkin pie spice.
6. **Serve:**
   - Pour the smoothie into glasses and serve immediately.

Enjoy your flavorful and comforting Pumpkin Spice Smoothie!

Ginger Pear Smoothie

Ingredients:

- 1 ripe pear (peeled, cored, and sliced)
- 1 banana (fresh or frozen)
- 1/2 teaspoon fresh grated ginger or 1/4 teaspoon ground ginger
- 1 cup (240 ml) milk (any kind: dairy or non-dairy like almond, soy, or oat milk)
- 1/2 cup (120 ml) Greek yogurt (plain or vanilla) or non-dairy yogurt
- 1 tablespoon honey or maple syrup (optional, adjust to taste)
- 1/2 teaspoon vanilla extract (optional)
- 1/2 cup ice (optional, if using fresh fruit or if you prefer a colder smoothie)

Instructions:

1. **Prepare the Ingredients:**
   - Peel, core, and slice the pear. Peel and slice the banana. If using fresh ginger, grate it finely. If using fresh fruit, consider adding ice for a thicker, colder smoothie.
2. **Blend:**
   - In a blender, combine the pear slices, banana, grated ginger or ground ginger, milk, Greek yogurt, and optional honey or maple syrup. Add vanilla extract if desired.
3. **Add Ice (if needed):**
   - If using fresh fruit or if you want a thicker, colder smoothie, add ice to the blender.
4. **Blend Until Smooth:**
   - Blend on high speed until the mixture is smooth and creamy. Adjust the consistency by adding more milk if needed.
5. **Taste and Adjust:**
   - Taste the smoothie and adjust sweetness or ginger flavor if needed by adding more honey/maple syrup or ginger.
6. **Serve:**
   - Pour the smoothie into glasses and serve immediately.

Enjoy your refreshing and invigorating Ginger Pear Smoothie!

Watermelon Mint Smoothie

Ingredients:

- 2 cups (300 g) watermelon chunks (seeds removed)
- 1/2 cup fresh mint leaves (about 10-12 leaves)
- 1 banana (fresh or frozen)
- 1 cup (240 ml) coconut water or plain water
- 1/2 cup (120 ml) Greek yogurt (plain or vanilla) or non-dairy yogurt
- 1 tablespoon honey or maple syrup (optional, adjust to taste)
- 1/2 cup ice (optional, if using fresh fruit or if you prefer a colder smoothie)

Instructions:

1. **Prepare the Ingredients:**
   - Cut the watermelon into chunks and remove any seeds. Peel and slice the banana. If you're using fresh mint, wash the leaves thoroughly. If using fresh fruit, consider adding ice for a thicker, colder smoothie.
2. **Blend:**
   - In a blender, combine the watermelon chunks, mint leaves, banana, coconut water or plain water, and Greek yogurt.
3. **Add Sweetener (if needed):**
   - Add honey or maple syrup if you prefer a sweeter smoothie.
4. **Add Ice (if needed):**
   - If using fresh fruit or if you want a colder, thicker smoothie, add ice to the blender.
5. **Blend Until Smooth:**
   - Blend on high speed until the mixture is smooth and creamy. Adjust the consistency by adding more coconut water or plain water if needed.
6. **Taste and Adjust:**
   - Taste the smoothie and adjust sweetness if needed by adding more honey or maple syrup.
7. **Serve:**
   - Pour the smoothie into glasses and serve immediately.

Enjoy your cool and refreshing Watermelon Mint Smoothie!

Strawberry Kiwi Smoothie

Ingredients:

- 1 cup (150 g) fresh or frozen strawberries (hulled)
- 2 ripe kiwis (peeled and sliced)
- 1 banana (fresh or frozen)
- 1 cup (240 ml) apple juice or coconut water
- 1/2 cup (120 ml) Greek yogurt (plain or vanilla) or non-dairy yogurt
- 1 tablespoon honey or maple syrup (optional, adjust to taste)
- 1/2 teaspoon vanilla extract (optional)
- 1/2 cup ice (optional, if using fresh fruit or if you prefer a colder smoothie)

Instructions:

1. **Prepare the Ingredients:**
   - Hull the strawberries and slice them if they are large. Peel and slice the kiwis. Peel and slice the banana. If using fresh fruit, you may want to add ice for a colder, thicker smoothie.
2. **Blend:**
   - In a blender, combine the strawberries, kiwis, banana, apple juice or coconut water, and Greek yogurt.
3. **Add Sweetener and Vanilla:**
   - Add honey or maple syrup if you prefer a sweeter smoothie. Add vanilla extract if desired.
4. **Add Ice (if needed):**
   - If using fresh fruit or if you want a thicker, colder smoothie, add ice to the blender.
5. **Blend Until Smooth:**
   - Blend on high speed until the mixture is smooth and creamy. Adjust the consistency by adding more apple juice or coconut water if needed.
6. **Taste and Adjust:**
   - Taste the smoothie and adjust sweetness if needed by adding more honey or maple syrup.
7. **Serve:**
   - Pour the smoothie into glasses and serve immediately.

Enjoy your refreshing and fruity Strawberry Kiwi Smoothie!

Mango Coconut Smoothie

Ingredients:

- 1 ripe mango, peeled and pitted
- 1 cup coconut milk (or coconut water for a lighter option)
- 1/2 cup Greek yogurt (optional for creaminess)
- 1 tablespoon honey or maple syrup (adjust to taste)
- 1/2 cup ice
- Optional: 1/4 cup shredded coconut or a handful of spinach for added nutrition

Instructions:

1. **Prepare the Mango**: Cut the mango into chunks.
2. **Blend**: In a blender, combine the mango chunks, coconut milk, Greek yogurt (if using), honey or maple syrup, and ice. Blend until smooth.
3. **Adjust Sweetness**: Taste the smoothie and add more honey or maple syrup if needed.
4. **Serve**: Pour into glasses and, if desired, sprinkle with shredded coconut on top for garnish.

Enjoy your tropical smoothie!

Chocolate Peanut Butter Smoothie

Ingredients:

- 1 banana (preferably frozen for a creamier texture)
- 2 tablespoons peanut butter
- 2 tablespoons cocoa powder (unsweetened)
- 1 cup milk (dairy or plant-based, like almond or oat milk)
- 1 tablespoon honey or maple syrup (adjust to taste)
- 1/2 cup Greek yogurt or a scoop of protein powder (optional for added creaminess and protein)
- 1/2 cup ice (optional for a thicker texture)

Instructions:

1. **Prepare Ingredients**: If your banana isn't frozen, you can use fresh, but frozen banana will make the smoothie creamier and colder.
2. **Blend**: In a blender, combine the banana, peanut butter, cocoa powder, milk, honey or maple syrup, and ice if using. Blend until smooth.
3. **Adjust Sweetness**: Taste the smoothie and add more honey or maple syrup if you like it sweeter.
4. **Optional Add-ins**: For extra creaminess, you can add Greek yogurt or a scoop of protein powder. Blend again if adding these.
5. **Serve**: Pour into a glass and enjoy immediately.

This smoothie combines the rich flavors of chocolate and peanut butter for a delicious and satisfying treat!

Beet Berry Smoothie

Ingredients:

- 1 small cooked beet (peeled and chopped; you can use pre-cooked or roast it yourself)
- 1 cup mixed berries (fresh or frozen; blueberries, strawberries, raspberries, etc.)
- 1 banana (for creaminess and sweetness)
- 1 cup spinach or kale (optional, for extra greens)
- 1 cup almond milk (or any milk of your choice)
- 1 tablespoon honey or maple syrup (optional, for added sweetness)
- 1/2 cup ice (optional, for a colder, thicker smoothie)

Instructions:

1. **Prepare the Beet**: If using raw beets, roast or steam them until tender, then peel and chop. If using pre-cooked beets, just chop them up.
2. **Blend**: Add the chopped beet, mixed berries, banana, spinach or kale (if using), almond milk, and honey or maple syrup to a blender. Blend until smooth.
3. **Adjust Sweetness**: Taste the smoothie and add more honey or maple syrup if desired.
4. **Optional**: If you prefer a thicker texture, add ice and blend again.
5. **Serve**: Pour into glasses and enjoy immediately!

This smoothie is packed with antioxidants, fiber, and a burst of natural sweetness.

Peach Ginger Smoothie

Ingredients:

- 2 ripe peaches, peeled and pitted (fresh or frozen)
- 1/2-inch piece of fresh ginger, peeled (or 1/2 teaspoon ground ginger)
- 1 banana (for creaminess)
- 1 cup Greek yogurt (or a dairy-free alternative)
- 1 cup almond milk (or any milk of your choice)
- 1 tablespoon honey or maple syrup (optional, for added sweetness)
- 1/2 cup ice (optional, for a thicker, colder smoothie)

Instructions:

1. **Prepare the Ginger**: If using fresh ginger, peel and finely grate or chop it. If using ground ginger, you can add it directly.
2. **Blend**: In a blender, combine the peaches, ginger, banana, Greek yogurt, almond milk, and honey or maple syrup. Blend until smooth.
3. **Adjust Sweetness**: Taste the smoothie and add more honey or maple syrup if needed.
4. **Optional**: For a thicker texture and extra chill, add ice and blend again.
5. **Serve**: Pour into glasses and enjoy immediately!

This smoothie combines the juicy sweetness of peaches with the warming, spicy notes of ginger, making it both refreshing and comforting.

Beet Berry Smoothie

Ingredients:

- 1 small cooked beet (peeled and chopped; you can use pre-cooked or roast it yourself)
- 1 cup mixed berries (fresh or frozen; blueberries, strawberries, raspberries, etc.)
- 1 banana (for creaminess and sweetness)
- 1 cup spinach or kale (optional, for extra greens)
- 1 cup almond milk (or any milk of your choice)
- 1 tablespoon honey or maple syrup (optional, for added sweetness)
- 1/2 cup ice (optional, for a colder, thicker smoothie)

Instructions:

1. **Prepare the Beet**: If using raw beets, roast or steam them until tender, then peel and chop. If using pre-cooked beets, just chop them up.
2. **Blend**: Add the chopped beet, mixed berries, banana, spinach or kale (if using), almond milk, and honey or maple syrup to a blender. Blend until smooth.
3. **Adjust Sweetness**: Taste the smoothie and add more honey or maple syrup if desired.
4. **Optional**: If you prefer a thicker texture, add ice and blend again.
5. **Serve**: Pour into glasses and enjoy immediately!

This smoothie is packed with antioxidants, fiber, and a burst of natural sweetness.

Peach Ginger Smoothie

Ingredients:

- 2 ripe peaches, peeled and pitted (fresh or frozen)
- 1/2-inch piece of fresh ginger, peeled (or 1/2 teaspoon ground ginger)
- 1 banana (for creaminess)
- 1 cup Greek yogurt (or a dairy-free alternative)
- 1 cup almond milk (or any milk of your choice)
- 1 tablespoon honey or maple syrup (optional, for added sweetness)
- 1/2 cup ice (optional, for a thicker, colder smoothie)

Instructions:

1. **Prepare the Ginger**: If using fresh ginger, peel and finely grate or chop it. If using ground ginger, you can add it directly.
2. **Blend**: In a blender, combine the peaches, ginger, banana, Greek yogurt, almond milk, and honey or maple syrup. Blend until smooth.
3. **Adjust Sweetness**: Taste the smoothie and add more honey or maple syrup if needed.
4. **Optional**: For a thicker texture and extra chill, add ice and blend again.
5. **Serve**: Pour into glasses and enjoy immediately!

This smoothie combines the juicy sweetness of peaches with the warming, spicy notes of ginger, making it both refreshing and comforting.

Green Tea Smoothie

Ingredients:

- 1 cup brewed green tea, cooled (or matcha powder mixed with water)
- 1 banana (for creaminess and sweetness)
- 1/2 cup Greek yogurt (or a dairy-free alternative)
- 1/2 cup spinach or kale (for extra greens)
- 1/2 cup frozen mango or berries (for added flavor and nutrition)
- 1 tablespoon honey or maple syrup (optional, for added sweetness)
- 1/2 cup ice (optional, for a colder, thicker smoothie)

Instructions:

1. **Brew Green Tea**: Brew 1 cup of green tea and let it cool to room temperature. Alternatively, mix 1-2 teaspoons of matcha powder with a small amount of water to create a matcha tea.
2. **Blend**: In a blender, combine the cooled green tea, banana, Greek yogurt, spinach or kale, frozen mango or berries, and honey or maple syrup. Blend until smooth.
3. **Adjust Sweetness**: Taste the smoothie and add more honey or maple syrup if needed.
4. **Optional**: For a thicker texture and extra chill, add ice and blend again.
5. **Serve**: Pour into glasses and enjoy immediately!

This smoothie is packed with antioxidants from the green tea and nutrients from the fruits and greens, making it both tasty and healthful.

Apple Spinach Smoothie

Ingredients:

- 1 apple (cored and sliced; you can leave the skin on for extra fiber)
- 1 cup fresh spinach (or a mix of spinach and kale)
- 1 banana (for creaminess and sweetness)
- 1/2 cup Greek yogurt (or a dairy-free alternative)
- 1/2 cup almond milk (or any milk of your choice)
- 1 tablespoon honey or maple syrup (optional, for added sweetness)
- 1/2 teaspoon lemon juice (optional, for a fresh zing)
- 1/2 cup ice (optional, for a colder, thicker smoothie)

Instructions:

1. **Prepare Ingredients**: Core and slice the apple. If you're using a very sweet apple, you might not need extra sweetener.
2. **Blend**: In a blender, combine the apple slices, spinach, banana, Greek yogurt, almond milk, and honey or maple syrup. Add lemon juice if using. Blend until smooth.
3. **Adjust Sweetness**: Taste the smoothie and adjust the sweetness with more honey or maple syrup if needed.
4. **Optional**: For a thicker texture and extra chill, add ice and blend again.
5. **Serve**: Pour into glasses and enjoy immediately!

This smoothie is rich in vitamins, minerals, and fiber, thanks to the combination of apple and spinach, and it's a great way to start your day or enjoy as a snack!

Pineapple Ginger Smoothie

Ingredients:

- 1 cup fresh or frozen pineapple chunks
- 1/2-inch piece of fresh ginger, peeled and grated (or 1/2 teaspoon ground ginger)
- 1 banana (for creaminess)
- 1/2 cup Greek yogurt (or a dairy-free alternative)
- 1/2 cup coconut water or almond milk (for a lighter base)
- 1 tablespoon honey or maple syrup (optional, for added sweetness)
- 1/2 cup ice (optional, for a colder, thicker smoothie)

Instructions:

1. **Prepare the Ginger**: Peel and grate the fresh ginger. If using ground ginger, you can add it directly.
2. **Blend**: In a blender, combine the pineapple chunks, grated ginger, banana, Greek yogurt, coconut water or almond milk, and honey or maple syrup. Blend until smooth.
3. **Adjust Sweetness**: Taste the smoothie and add more honey or maple syrup if needed.
4. **Optional**: For a thicker texture and extra chill, add ice and blend again.
5. **Serve**: Pour into glasses and enjoy immediately!

This smoothie not only has a great balance of tropical sweetness and spicy warmth but also provides a boost of vitamins and digestive benefits from the pineapple and ginger.

Cucumber Melon Smoothie

Ingredients:

- 1 cup honeydew melon or cantaloupe, peeled, seeded, and chopped
- 1/2 cucumber, peeled and chopped
- 1/2 cup Greek yogurt or a dairy-free alternative
- 1 tablespoon honey or maple syrup (optional, for added sweetness)
- 1/2 cup water or coconut water (for a lighter base)
- 1/2 cup ice (optional, for a colder, thicker smoothie)
- Fresh mint leaves (optional, for garnish and added freshness)

Instructions:

1. **Prepare Ingredients**: Chop the honeydew melon or cantaloupe and cucumber into chunks. If using a whole cucumber, peel it and remove the seeds if desired for a smoother texture.
2. **Blend**: In a blender, combine the melon chunks, cucumber, Greek yogurt, honey or maple syrup, and water or coconut water. Blend until smooth.
3. **Adjust Sweetness**: Taste the smoothie and add more honey or maple syrup if needed.
4. **Optional**: For a thicker texture and extra chill, add ice and blend again.
5. **Serve**: Pour into glasses and garnish with fresh mint leaves if desired.

This smoothie is hydrating, low in calories, and packed with vitamins, making it a great choice for a refreshing snack or light meal.

Raspberry Banana Smoothie

Ingredients:

- 1 cup fresh or frozen raspberries
- 1 banana (preferably frozen for a creamier texture)
- 1/2 cup Greek yogurt or a dairy-free alternative
- 1/2 cup almond milk or any milk of your choice
- 1 tablespoon honey or maple syrup (optional, for added sweetness)
- 1/2 cup ice (optional, for a thicker, colder smoothie)

Instructions:

1. **Prepare Ingredients**: If your banana isn't frozen, you can use fresh, but frozen banana will make the smoothie creamier and colder.
2. **Blend**: In a blender, combine the raspberries, banana, Greek yogurt, almond milk, and honey or maple syrup. Blend until smooth.
3. **Adjust Sweetness**: Taste the smoothie and add more honey or maple syrup if needed.
4. **Optional**: For a thicker texture and extra chill, add ice and blend again.
5. **Serve**: Pour into glasses and enjoy immediately!

This smoothie is packed with antioxidants from the raspberries and offers a creamy, satisfying texture from the banana and yogurt.

Avocado Matcha Smoothie

Ingredients:

- 1 ripe avocado (peeled and pitted)
- 1 teaspoon matcha powder
- 1 banana (for sweetness and creaminess)
- 1 cup spinach or kale (optional, for extra greens)
- 1 cup almond milk (or any milk of your choice)
- 1 tablespoon honey or maple syrup (optional, for added sweetness)
- 1/2 cup ice (optional, for a colder, thicker smoothie)

Instructions:

1. **Prepare the Avocado**: Peel and pit the avocado, then scoop the flesh into the blender.
2. **Blend**: Add the matcha powder, banana, spinach or kale (if using), almond milk, and honey or maple syrup to the blender. Blend until smooth.
3. **Adjust Sweetness**: Taste the smoothie and add more honey or maple syrup if needed.
4. **Optional**: For a thicker texture and extra chill, add ice and blend again.
5. **Serve**: Pour into glasses and enjoy immediately.

This smoothie is packed with healthy fats from the avocado, antioxidants from the matcha, and a boost of vitamins from the greens and banana, making it both delicious and nourishing.

Berry Almond Smoothie

Ingredients:

- 1 cup mixed berries (fresh or frozen; blueberries, strawberries, raspberries, etc.)
- 1 tablespoon almond butter (or 1/4 cup almonds if you prefer to blend them)
- 1 banana (for creaminess and natural sweetness)
- 1/2 cup Greek yogurt or a dairy-free alternative
- 1 cup almond milk (or any milk of your choice)
- 1 tablespoon honey or maple syrup (optional, for added sweetness)
- 1/2 cup ice (optional, for a thicker, colder smoothie)

Instructions:

1. **Prepare Ingredients**: If using almonds instead of almond butter, you may want to blend them first to a fine powder before adding the rest of the ingredients.
2. **Blend**: In a blender, combine the mixed berries, almond butter (or ground almonds), banana, Greek yogurt, almond milk, and honey or maple syrup. Blend until smooth.
3. **Adjust Sweetness**: Taste the smoothie and add more honey or maple syrup if desired.
4. **Optional**: For a thicker texture and extra chill, add ice and blend again.
5. **Serve**: Pour into glasses and enjoy immediately.

This smoothie is packed with antioxidants from the berries, healthy fats from the almonds, and protein from the Greek yogurt, making it a well-rounded and satisfying drink.

Tropical Fruit Smoothie

Ingredients:

- 1 cup pineapple chunks (fresh or frozen)
- 1 cup mango chunks (fresh or frozen)
- 1 banana (for creaminess)
- 1/2 cup coconut yogurt or Greek yogurt (optional, for added creaminess)
- 1 cup coconut water or almond milk (for a lighter base)
- 1 tablespoon honey or maple syrup (optional, for added sweetness)
- 1/2 cup ice (optional, for a thicker, colder smoothie)
- 1 tablespoon chia seeds or flaxseeds (optional, for added nutrition)

Instructions:

1. **Prepare Ingredients**: If you're using fresh pineapple and mango, peel and chop them into chunks. If using frozen fruit, you can skip the ice.
2. **Blend**: In a blender, combine the pineapple chunks, mango chunks, banana, coconut yogurt (if using), coconut water or almond milk, and honey or maple syrup. Blend until smooth.
3. **Adjust Sweetness**: Taste the smoothie and add more honey or maple syrup if needed.
4. **Optional**: For a thicker texture and extra chill, add ice and blend again. You can also add chia seeds or flaxseeds for extra fiber and omega-3s.
5. **Serve**: Pour into glasses and enjoy immediately!

This smoothie combines the tropical flavors of pineapple and mango with the creamy texture of banana and coconut, making it a delightful and nutritious treat.

Date Almond Smoothie

Ingredients:

- 4-6 Medjool dates, pitted
- 1/4 cup almond butter (or 1/4 cup almonds if you prefer to blend them)
- 1 banana (for creaminess)
- 1 cup almond milk (or any milk of your choice)
- 1/2 cup Greek yogurt or a dairy-free alternative (optional, for added creaminess)
- 1/2 teaspoon vanilla extract (optional, for extra flavor)
- 1/2 cup ice (optional, for a thicker, colder smoothie)
- A pinch of cinnamon (optional, for added warmth)

Instructions:

1. **Prepare Dates**: If the dates are not soft, soak them in warm water for about 10 minutes to soften, then drain.
2. **Blend**: In a blender, combine the dates, almond butter (or ground almonds), banana, almond milk, Greek yogurt (if using), and vanilla extract. Blend until smooth.
3. **Adjust Sweetness**: Taste the smoothie and add more dates or a bit of honey if you prefer it sweeter.
4. **Optional**: For a thicker texture and extra chill, add ice and blend again. You can also add a pinch of cinnamon for extra flavor.
5. **Serve**: Pour into glasses and enjoy immediately!

This smoothie is naturally sweetened with dates and packed with protein and healthy fats from the almonds, making it a satisfying and nutritious choice.

Papaya Pineapple Smoothie

Ingredients:

- 1 cup papaya, peeled, seeded, and chopped
- 1 cup pineapple chunks (fresh or frozen)
- 1 banana (for added creaminess and sweetness)
- 1/2 cup Greek yogurt or a dairy-free alternative (optional, for extra creaminess)
- 1 cup coconut water or almond milk (for a lighter base)
- 1 tablespoon honey or maple syrup (optional, for added sweetness)
- 1/2 cup ice (optional, for a thicker, colder smoothie)
- Fresh mint leaves (optional, for garnish)

Instructions:

1. **Prepare Ingredients**: Peel and chop the papaya. If you're using fresh pineapple, peel and chop it into chunks. If using frozen pineapple, you can skip the ice.
2. **Blend**: In a blender, combine the papaya, pineapple, banana, Greek yogurt (if using), and coconut water or almond milk. Blend until smooth.
3. **Adjust Sweetness**: Taste the smoothie and add honey or maple syrup if needed, blending again to mix.
4. **Optional**: For a thicker texture and extra chill, add ice and blend again.
5. **Serve**: Pour into glasses and garnish with fresh mint leaves if desired.

This smoothie is packed with vitamins and tropical flavors, making it a perfect way to refresh and energize your day!

Coconut Vanilla Smoothie

Ingredients:

- 1 cup coconut milk (or coconut water for a lighter option)
- 1 banana (for creaminess)
- 1/2 cup Greek yogurt or a dairy-free alternative (optional, for added creaminess)
- 1 tablespoon vanilla extract
- 1 tablespoon honey or maple syrup (optional, for added sweetness)
- 1/2 cup ice (optional, for a thicker, colder smoothie)
- Shredded coconut or a sprinkle of cinnamon (optional, for garnish)

Instructions:

1. **Blend**: In a blender, combine the coconut milk, banana, Greek yogurt (if using), vanilla extract, and honey or maple syrup. Blend until smooth.
2. **Adjust Sweetness**: Taste the smoothie and add more honey or maple syrup if needed.
3. **Optional**: For a thicker texture and extra chill, add ice and blend again.
4. **Serve**: Pour into glasses and garnish with shredded coconut or a sprinkle of cinnamon if desired.

This smoothie is rich in coconut flavor with a hint of vanilla, offering a creamy and delightful taste that's both satisfying and refreshing.

Mixed Berry Smoothie

Ingredients:

- 1 cup mixed berries (fresh or frozen; e.g., strawberries, blueberries, raspberries, blackberries)
- 1 banana (for creaminess and natural sweetness)
- 1/2 cup Greek yogurt or a dairy-free alternative (optional, for extra creaminess)
- 1 cup almond milk or any milk of your choice
- 1 tablespoon honey or maple syrup (optional, for added sweetness)
- 1/2 cup ice (optional, for a thicker, colder smoothie)

Instructions:

1. **Blend**: In a blender, combine the mixed berries, banana, Greek yogurt (if using), almond milk, and honey or maple syrup. Blend until smooth.
2. **Adjust Sweetness**: Taste the smoothie and add more honey or maple syrup if needed, then blend again to combine.
3. **Optional**: For a thicker texture and extra chill, add ice and blend until smooth.
4. **Serve**: Pour into glasses and enjoy immediately!

This smoothie is packed with vitamins, antioxidants, and fiber from the berries, making it a healthy and tasty choice for breakfast or a snack.

Cantaloupe Mint Smoothie

Ingredients:

- 1 cup cantaloupe, peeled, seeded, and chopped
- 1/2 cup fresh mint leaves
- 1 banana (for added creaminess)
- 1/2 cup Greek yogurt or a dairy-free alternative (optional, for extra creaminess)
- 1 cup coconut water or almond milk (for a lighter base)
- 1 tablespoon honey or maple syrup (optional, for added sweetness)
- 1/2 cup ice (optional, for a colder, thicker smoothie)

Instructions:

1. **Prepare Ingredients**: Peel and chop the cantaloupe into chunks. If your banana isn't frozen, you can use fresh, but frozen banana will make the smoothie creamier and colder.
2. **Blend**: In a blender, combine the cantaloupe chunks, fresh mint leaves, banana, Greek yogurt (if using), and coconut water or almond milk. Blend until smooth.
3. **Adjust Sweetness**: Taste the smoothie and add honey or maple syrup if needed, then blend again to combine.
4. **Optional**: For a thicker texture and extra chill, add ice and blend until smooth.
5. **Serve**: Pour into glasses and enjoy immediately!

This smoothie combines the sweetness of cantaloupe with the refreshing notes of mint, making it a delightful and hydrating choice.

Strawberry Chia Smoothie

Ingredients:

- 1 cup fresh or frozen strawberries
- 1 banana (for creaminess and sweetness)
- 1 tablespoon chia seeds
- 1/2 cup Greek yogurt or a dairy-free alternative (optional, for extra creaminess)
- 1 cup almond milk or any milk of your choice
- 1 tablespoon honey or maple syrup (optional, for added sweetness)
- 1/2 cup ice (optional, for a colder, thicker smoothie)

Instructions:

1. **Prepare Chia Seeds**: For best results, let the chia seeds soak in 2 tablespoons of water or almond milk for about 10 minutes to form a gel-like consistency. This step is optional but helps to make the smoothie smoother.
2. **Blend**: In a blender, combine the strawberries, banana, chia seeds, Greek yogurt (if using), and almond milk. Blend until smooth.
3. **Adjust Sweetness**: Taste the smoothie and add honey or maple syrup if needed, then blend again to combine.
4. **Optional**: For a thicker texture and extra chill, add ice and blend until smooth.
5. **Serve**: Pour into glasses and enjoy immediately!

This smoothie is rich in antioxidants from the strawberries and omega-3 fatty acids from the chia seeds, making it a tasty and healthful option for any time of day.

Mango Lime Smoothie

Ingredients:

- 1 cup mango chunks (fresh or frozen)
- 1/2 cup Greek yogurt or a dairy-free alternative (optional, for extra creaminess)
- Juice of 1 lime (about 2 tablespoons)
- 1 tablespoon honey or maple syrup (optional, for added sweetness)
- 1 cup coconut water or almond milk (for a lighter base)
- 1/2 cup ice (optional, for a thicker, colder smoothie)
- Lime zest (optional, for garnish)

Instructions:

1. **Blend**: In a blender, combine the mango chunks, Greek yogurt (if using), lime juice, honey or maple syrup, and coconut water or almond milk. Blend until smooth.
2. **Adjust Sweetness**: Taste the smoothie and add more honey or maple syrup if needed, then blend again to combine.
3. **Optional**: For a thicker texture and extra chill, add ice and blend until smooth.
4. **Serve**: Pour into glasses and garnish with a sprinkle of lime zest if desired. Enjoy immediately!

This smoothie is packed with the vibrant flavors of mango and lime, offering a delightful tropical taste that's both refreshing and satisfying.

Pineapple Kale Smoothie

Ingredients:

- 1 cup pineapple chunks (fresh or frozen)
- 1 cup kale leaves, stems removed (packed)
- 1 banana (for creaminess and added sweetness)
- 1/2 cup Greek yogurt or a dairy-free alternative (optional, for extra creaminess)
- 1 cup coconut water or almond milk (for a lighter base)
- 1 tablespoon honey or maple syrup (optional, for added sweetness)
- 1/2 cup ice (optional, for a thicker, colder smoothie)

Instructions:

1. **Prepare Kale**: Wash and remove the stems from the kale leaves.
2. **Blend**: In a blender, combine the pineapple chunks, kale leaves, banana, Greek yogurt (if using), and coconut water or almond milk. Blend until smooth.
3. **Adjust Sweetness**: Taste the smoothie and add honey or maple syrup if needed, then blend again to combine.
4. **Optional**: For a thicker texture and extra chill, add ice and blend until smooth.
5. **Serve**: Pour into glasses and enjoy immediately!

This smoothie is packed with vitamins, minerals, and antioxidants from both the pineapple and kale, making it a nutritious and delicious choice for a refreshing drink.

Chocolate Cherry Smoothie

Ingredients:

- 1 cup frozen cherries (pitted)
- 1 banana (for creaminess and sweetness)
- 2 tablespoons cocoa powder (unsweetened)
- 1/2 cup Greek yogurt or a dairy-free alternative (optional, for extra creaminess)
- 1 cup almond milk or any milk of your choice
- 1 tablespoon honey or maple syrup (optional, for added sweetness)
- 1/2 cup ice (optional, for a thicker, colder smoothie)

Instructions:

1. **Blend**: In a blender, combine the frozen cherries, banana, cocoa powder, Greek yogurt (if using), and almond milk. Blend until smooth.
2. **Adjust Sweetness**: Taste the smoothie and add honey or maple syrup if needed, then blend again to combine.
3. **Optional**: For a thicker texture and extra chill, add ice and blend until smooth.
4. **Serve**: Pour into glasses and enjoy immediately.

This smoothie is rich in antioxidants from the cherries and cocoa, while the banana and yogurt add creaminess and natural sweetness, making it a satisfying and nutritious treat.

Peach Blueberry Smoothie

Ingredients:

- 1 cup fresh or frozen peaches, peeled and sliced
- 1 cup fresh or frozen blueberries
- 1 banana (for creaminess and added sweetness)
- 1/2 cup Greek yogurt or a dairy-free alternative (optional, for extra creaminess)
- 1 cup almond milk or any milk of your choice
- 1 tablespoon honey or maple syrup (optional, for added sweetness)
- 1/2 cup ice (optional, for a thicker, colder smoothie)

Instructions:

1. **Blend**: In a blender, combine the peaches, blueberries, banana, Greek yogurt (if using), and almond milk. Blend until smooth.
2. **Adjust Sweetness**: Taste the smoothie and add honey or maple syrup if desired, then blend again to combine.
3. **Optional**: For a thicker texture and extra chill, add ice and blend until smooth.
4. **Serve**: Pour into glasses and enjoy immediately!

This smoothie is packed with antioxidants, vitamins, and natural sweetness from the fruits, making it a refreshing and healthful choice.

Green Apple Smoothie

Ingredients:

- 1 green apple, cored and sliced (leave the skin on for extra fiber)
- 1/2 cup spinach or kale (optional, for added greens)
- 1 banana (for creaminess and sweetness)
- 1/2 cup Greek yogurt or a dairy-free alternative (optional, for extra creaminess)
- 1 cup almond milk or any milk of your choice
- 1 tablespoon honey or maple syrup (optional, for added sweetness)
- 1/2 cup ice (optional, for a colder, thicker smoothie)

Instructions:

1. **Prepare the Apple**: Core and slice the green apple. If using fresh spinach or kale, wash and chop it.
2. **Blend**: In a blender, combine the apple slices, spinach or kale (if using), banana, Greek yogurt (if using), and almond milk. Blend until smooth.
3. **Adjust Sweetness**: Taste the smoothie and add honey or maple syrup if needed, then blend again to combine.
4. **Optional**: For a thicker texture and extra chill, add ice and blend until smooth.
5. **Serve**: Pour into glasses and enjoy immediately!

This smoothie is packed with fiber, vitamins, and minerals, making it a refreshing and healthful choice for any time of day.

Spiced Pear Smoothie

Ingredients:

- 1 ripe pear, cored and sliced (no need to peel if you prefer extra fiber)
- 1 banana (for creaminess and natural sweetness)
- 1/2 cup Greek yogurt or a dairy-free alternative (optional, for extra creaminess)
- 1/2 cup almond milk or any milk of your choice
- 1/2 teaspoon ground cinnamon
- 1/4 teaspoon ground nutmeg
- 1 tablespoon honey or maple syrup (optional, for added sweetness)
- 1/2 cup ice (optional, for a thicker, colder smoothie)

Instructions:

1. **Prepare the Pear**: Core and slice the pear. If using a very sweet pear, you might not need extra sweetener.
2. **Blend**: In a blender, combine the pear slices, banana, Greek yogurt (if using), almond milk, ground cinnamon, and ground nutmeg. Blend until smooth.
3. **Adjust Sweetness**: Taste the smoothie and add honey or maple syrup if needed, then blend again to combine.
4. **Optional**: For a thicker texture and extra chill, add ice and blend until smooth.
5. **Serve**: Pour into glasses and enjoy immediately.

This smoothie offers a lovely combination of fruity sweetness and cozy spices, making it a comforting and nutritious choice.

Almond Joy Smoothie

Ingredients:

- 1 banana (for creaminess and sweetness)
- 1 cup almond milk or any milk of your choice
- 2 tablespoons cocoa powder (unsweetened)
- 1 tablespoon almond butter or 1/4 cup almonds
- 1/4 cup shredded coconut (unsweetened)
- 1 tablespoon honey or maple syrup (optional, for added sweetness)
- 1/2 cup ice (optional, for a thicker, colder smoothie)
- Almonds and shredded coconut for garnish (optional)

Instructions:

1. **Blend**: In a blender, combine the banana, almond milk, cocoa powder, almond butter (or almonds), shredded coconut, and honey or maple syrup. Blend until smooth.
2. **Adjust Sweetness**: Taste the smoothie and add more honey or maple syrup if desired, then blend again to combine.
3. **Optional**: For a thicker texture and extra chill, add ice and blend until smooth.
4. **Serve**: Pour into glasses and garnish with extra almonds and shredded coconut if desired.

This smoothie is packed with the flavors of chocolate and coconut, with the added richness of almonds, making it a tasty and satisfying treat.

Coconut Pineapple Smoothie

Ingredients:

- 1 cup pineapple chunks (fresh or frozen)
- 1/2 cup coconut yogurt or Greek yogurt (optional, for extra creaminess)
- 1/2 cup coconut milk or coconut water (for a lighter base)
- 1 banana (for added creaminess and sweetness)
- 1 tablespoon honey or maple syrup (optional, for added sweetness)
- 1/2 cup ice (optional, for a thicker, colder smoothie)
- Shredded coconut for garnish (optional)

Instructions:

1. **Blend**: In a blender, combine the pineapple chunks, coconut yogurt (if using), coconut milk or coconut water, and banana. Blend until smooth.
2. **Adjust Sweetness**: Taste the smoothie and add honey or maple syrup if needed, then blend again to combine.
3. **Optional**: For a thicker texture and extra chill, add ice and blend until smooth.
4. **Serve**: Pour into glasses and garnish with shredded coconut if desired.

This smoothie is not only refreshing but also packed with tropical flavors and a creamy texture, making it a delightful choice for a snack or breakfast.

Berry Protein Smoothie

Ingredients:

- 1 cup mixed berries (fresh or frozen; e.g., strawberries, blueberries, raspberries)
- 1 banana (for creaminess and natural sweetness)
- 1 scoop protein powder (whey, plant-based, or any protein powder of your choice)
- 1/2 cup Greek yogurt or a dairy-free alternative (optional, for extra creaminess)
- 1 cup almond milk or any milk of your choice
- 1 tablespoon honey or maple syrup (optional, for added sweetness)
- 1/2 cup ice (optional, for a thicker, colder smoothie)

Instructions:

1. **Blend**: In a blender, combine the mixed berries, banana, protein powder, Greek yogurt (if using), and almond milk. Blend until smooth.
2. **Adjust Sweetness**: Taste the smoothie and add honey or maple syrup if needed, then blend again to combine.
3. **Optional**: For a thicker texture and extra chill, add ice and blend until smooth.
4. **Serve**: Pour into glasses and enjoy immediately!

This smoothie is packed with antioxidants from the berries, protein for muscle repair and satiety, and a creamy texture from the yogurt and banana, making it a balanced and delicious option for a post-workout snack or a nutritious breakfast.

Kiwi Coconut Smoothie

Ingredients:

- 2-3 kiwis, peeled and chopped
- 1/2 cup coconut yogurt or Greek yogurt (optional, for extra creaminess)
- 1/2 cup coconut milk or coconut water
- 1 banana (for added creaminess and sweetness)
- 1 tablespoon honey or maple syrup (optional, for added sweetness)
- 1/2 cup ice (optional, for a thicker, colder smoothie)
- Shredded coconut for garnish (optional)

Instructions:

1. **Prepare the Kiwi**: Peel and chop the kiwis.
2. **Blend**: In a blender, combine the chopped kiwi, coconut yogurt (if using), coconut milk or coconut water, and banana. Blend until smooth.
3. **Adjust Sweetness**: Taste the smoothie and add honey or maple syrup if needed, then blend again to combine.
4. **Optional**: For a thicker texture and extra chill, add ice and blend until smooth.
5. **Serve**: Pour into glasses and garnish with shredded coconut if desired.

This smoothie is packed with vitamin C from the kiwi and the rich flavor of coconut, making it a refreshing and nutritious choice.

Avocado Pineapple Smoothie

Ingredients:

- 1 ripe avocado, peeled and pitted
- 1 cup pineapple chunks (fresh or frozen)
- 1 banana (for added creaminess and natural sweetness)
- 1/2 cup Greek yogurt or a dairy-free alternative (optional, for extra creaminess)
- 1 cup coconut water or almond milk (for a lighter base)
- 1 tablespoon honey or maple syrup (optional, for added sweetness)
- 1/2 cup ice (optional, for a thicker, colder smoothie)

Instructions:

1. **Prepare Ingredients**: Peel and pit the avocado. If using fresh pineapple, chop it into chunks. If using frozen pineapple, you can skip the ice.
2. **Blend**: In a blender, combine the avocado, pineapple chunks, banana, Greek yogurt (if using), and coconut water or almond milk. Blend until smooth.
3. **Adjust Sweetness**: Taste the smoothie and add honey or maple syrup if needed, then blend again to combine.
4. **Optional**: For a thicker texture and extra chill, add ice and blend until smooth.
5. **Serve**: Pour into glasses and enjoy immediately.

This smoothie combines the creamy richness of avocado with the tropical sweetness of pineapple, creating a delicious and satisfying drink that's packed with healthy fats and vitamins.

Berry Citrus Smoothie

Ingredients:

- 1 cup mixed berries (fresh or frozen; e.g., strawberries, blueberries, raspberries)
- 1 orange, peeled and segmented
- 1/2 cup Greek yogurt or a dairy-free alternative (optional, for extra creaminess)
- 1 banana (for added creaminess and natural sweetness)
- 1 cup almond milk or any milk of your choice
- 1 tablespoon honey or maple syrup (optional, for added sweetness)
- 1/2 cup ice (optional, for a thicker, colder smoothie)

Instructions:

1. **Prepare Citrus**: Peel and segment the orange.
2. **Blend**: In a blender, combine the mixed berries, orange segments, Greek yogurt (if using), banana, and almond milk. Blend until smooth.
3. **Adjust Sweetness**: Taste the smoothie and add honey or maple syrup if needed, then blend again to combine.
4. **Optional**: For a thicker texture and extra chill, add ice and blend until smooth.
5. **Serve**: Pour into glasses and enjoy immediately.

This smoothie is packed with antioxidants from the berries and vitamin C from the citrus, offering a delightful and nutritious boost.

Ginger Peach Smoothie

Ingredients:

- 1 cup peaches (fresh or frozen, peeled and sliced)
- 1/2 teaspoon fresh ginger, grated (or 1/4 teaspoon ground ginger)
- 1 banana (for added creaminess and natural sweetness)
- 1/2 cup Greek yogurt or a dairy-free alternative (optional, for extra creaminess)
- 1 cup almond milk or any milk of your choice
- 1 tablespoon honey or maple syrup (optional, for added sweetness)
- 1/2 cup ice (optional, for a thicker, colder smoothie)

Instructions:

1. **Prepare Ingredients**: If using fresh peaches, peel and slice them. If using frozen peaches, you can skip the ice. Grate fresh ginger or measure ground ginger.
2. **Blend**: In a blender, combine the peaches, grated ginger, banana, Greek yogurt (if using), and almond milk. Blend until smooth.
3. **Adjust Sweetness**: Taste the smoothie and add honey or maple syrup if needed, then blend again to combine.
4. **Optional**: For a thicker texture and extra chill, add ice and blend until smooth.
5. **Serve**: Pour into glasses and enjoy immediately.

This smoothie provides a delightful balance of peach sweetness and ginger spice, offering a refreshing and nutritious drink with a hint of warmth.

Printed in the USA
CPSIA information can be obtained
at www.ICGtesting.com
CBHW080316041024
15321CB00067B/3475